T0195682

BARK-LEE:
The Making of a Champion

ROBERT STERN

authorHOUSE

AuthorHouse™
1663 Liberty Drive
Bloomington, IN 47403
www.authorhouse.com
Phone: 833-262-8899

Published by AuthorHouse 09/07/2021

ISBN: 978-1-6655-3680-6 (sc)

Library of Congress Control Number: 2021917764

Print information available on the last page.

INTRODUCTION

My wife and I had been waiting for more than a year to adopt a puppy. Our previous dog, Brody, a wheaten terrier, had passed away after 12 years of playful fun and warm memories. After our experience with Brody only another wheaten would do. Since the breed is not that common it had taken a long time to find our next pet.

We attended dog shows and networked to find a breeder with a litter ready for adoption. Finally we found Sheri a mere 150 miles down the interstate from home. My wife and I settled down on the living room couch while Sheri fetched the cutest 9 week old puppy and announced "There's your pup".

We looked at each other and smiled. It brought back fond memories of Brody the day we picked him up to take him home.

Just then another dog leaped on the couch and began licking my face. "That's Justin. He's two years old", said Sheri.

Justin was not about to quit licking. That long pink tongue slobbered all over my face from ear to ear. My chin was dripping with dog saliva. "Justin is a show dog," Sheri explained. "He just won his first championship in the ring," then paused. "You can take him if you prefer".

In case I had not understood the face lathering, Justin jumped off the couch and stared at me while his tail began wagging as if it were a windshield wiper fighting a tropical rain storm. My wife and I looked at each other. It was obvious that Justin was hoping to be adopted and to ride home with us. I hesitated for a second before announcing, "We're taking Justin. But we already picked a name for our next dog. We are going to call him Bark-Lee".

Sheri smiled. Then she told us the story that encouraged me to write this book.

CHAPTER 1
The whelping

◇◇

It was a dark and stormy night. The Campbells, Pamela and Stuart, finished dinner quickly and piled the dishes in the dishwasher. The storm rattled the windowpanes as sheets of rain shook the glass. Lightning flashed across the landscape followed each time by a thunderclap, each seemingly louder than the last.

Jenny and Fitz, the Campbell's terriers cowered in separate corners of the room. Each thunderclap was followed by a series of barks from Fitz. Jenny just whimpered. Jenny could hardly walk, her belly, full of puppies waiting to be born, almost scraping the parquet floor. Finally she slunk into her basket and curled her tail around her rounded form.

Stuart looked over at Jenny." I think she's due tonight. We had better prepare for the whelping".

"First time is always tricky", said Pamela. "Shouldn't we call the vet?".

"I doubt he would come in this weather. The highway is sure to be flooded and the state patrol will be rerouting traffic. We can handle this ourselves."

Suddenly the lights went out in the living room and throughout the house. Lightning zig zagged through the trees at the back of the lawn followed almost immediately by the loudest thunderclap yet. Fitz jumped onto the couch and nestled his body next to Stuart. No longer barking he emitted a series of low level whines.

Pamela got up, went into the kitchen and came back with two lit candles which she set on the coffee table. Stuart reached for the small transistor radio that he kept on the bookshelf. He tuned into the 24 hour news station, the only source of news now that the storm had cut the electricity to the house.

A voice crackled over the air waves. "Storm warnings in effect for the next six hours. Wind gusts up to 60 miles an hour. Local flooding could be severe. The state patrol is asking all residence of Garden City to stay indoors."

"I doubt the electricity will come back on tonight," said Stuart. "I'm going to the garage to get that lantern we use on our camping trip. Come in handy tonight."

Jenny gave a sigh, got up and immediately settled back

in her cushioned basket, obviously trying to get comfortable but without much success.

Around midnight the first puppy emerged. Suddenly it wasn't just Jenny in the basket but a small furry bundle that lay inert at her side. The puppy looked like he was enveloped in a thin layer of shrink wrapped clear plastic. Jenny instinctively knew what to do. She started licking the membrane that covered the pup. Two minutes later all traces of the coating were gone. A small wet furry bundle, no bigger than a bread roll began to breathe and wiggle.

By the time Jenny had finished cleaning off her first born puppy number two emerged. Jenny immediately went back to cleaning up the new arrival.

Stuart and Pamela sat and watched this miracle of birth. The lantern shone a ghostly light on the scene. Fitz remained in his corner totally uninvolved with his new offspring. Jenny needed no help although Pamela and Stuart were ready should any of the puppies need to be cleaned off. The couple had taken Jenny for an ultrasound which had revealed that she was carrying seven puppies. Sure enough the seventh and last pup was born soon after 2 AM. All seven were nestled against Jenny's warm torso. By then the storm had subsided. Exhausted, Stuart and Pamela let Fitz out in the backyard for a brief run and then slumped off to bed.

CHAPTER 2
The Awakening

◇◇◇

The first thing I remember was someone was standing on my head. Well at least two paws were pressing down on my scalp, the other two were over my eyes blocking my vision. I shook myself loose and noticed I was surrounded by a mass of brown and black fur that seemed to belong to a wriggling sea of bodies surging in constant motion. Until that day I couldn't see anything, just felt a jostling that never stopped. I looked down at myself and noticed I looked just like those other little brown sausages. There must be a reason why we all look alike.

I felt a little twinge in my middle, sort of like an empty spot that needed filling. I looked around. There was a nice sweet smell coming from this big smooth sack. The body that had been standing on my head tumbled forward and headed to what looked like a spigot sticking out of the sack. I followed. There were several spigots in a row and the smell was coming from them. I licked the spigot. It tasted sweet so I put it in my mouth and sucked. The warm liquid was delicious. Soon that empty feeling was gone.

Those other little sausages – I guess I am one of them too – seemed to spend a lot of time sucking on those spigots. We were all confined to a big box. No way out over those high walls so when we were not sleeping we were trying to climb over each other. It made no sense to me but since everyone was doing it I played along.

It was fun: Wake up, suck on the spigot, climb on someone's back, roll off, get trod on, squeal for help, scamper into a corner, go get another drink, fall asleep and repeat the whole process.

I noticed there were six others just like me. And there was this other one who owned the spigots and once in a while would lash out with an enormous paw. Looked just like mine except a whole lot bigger. It was just a bigger version of us smaller fry. That paw smack never hurt, it just rolled us over and after a while we got to understand that there were some things that were off limits, whatever that means. We just knew that when we did that the big paw was about to swat.

I liked being around Big Paws. I later found out she was our mom and she took care of us. What I liked best was when she used her enormous tongue to smooth my hair. Almost every day we got licked by our mom. Some of the others didn't care for that and tried to hide from her but I loved the slightly coarse tongue making my hair clean and bright.

One thing I did notice is that whereas all seven of us looked alike, her hair was much lighter. Maybe she will turn dark after a while so we will all look the same.

CHAPTER 3

Decision Time

◇◇◇

"It's been eight weeks and some of the pups are due to leave next week," said Pamela. "Do you think it's time we called Howard to pick … the one?"

"Probably a good idea before we send the first pup to his new home. We don't want to give up a potential Best In Show"

"Harry and Lisa are coming on Saturday to pick up their puppy so I had better call Howard and have him come over on Friday."

"I have a meeting I have to attend in the afternoon but you and Howard can make the decision, can't you?" asked Stuart.

"No problem. Any case, Howard just gives us his opinion and then we decide."

A few days later there was Howard at the door. Pamela let him in and escorted him to the box where the puppies were frolicking.

"Looks like an energetic bunch. Bet mom will be relieved to get rid of that lot", said Howard.

"Well, they are all just about weaned except the one with the yellow ribbon. She is the runt and it will be a couple of weeks before we let her go".

Howard put on his rubber gloves and reached into the pile of squirming fur balls. He ignored the squeals of protest, the thrashing of little paws and the wriggling of brown bodies. One at a time he lifted each puppy to give it a thorough examination. Then he went back to a couple which he examined a second time.

He opened each dog's mouth, examined the teeth, checked the ears, lifted the tail and then took some measurements with a short ruler he hauled out of his rear pocket.

"I think either the red ribbon guy or the blue ribbon gal have the best prospects in the show ring. Personally I would go with Mr. Red," exclaimed Howard.

"Thanks Howard," replied Pamela, "I'll discuss it with Stuart tonight. Just send me the bill for your service and we'll mail you a check next week."

That night Pamela and Stuart went out for their usual Friday night dinner with their friends Kate and Hayden. That couple had owned terriers for years from the time their children were growing up. Now with an empty nest, their children gone, the couple decided they wanted to travel more and so were dogless for the first time in decades. Still they enjoyed visiting with the Campbells and playing with their dogs.

"That red ribbon dog is so friendly. I love playing with him. He scrambles up my arm, perches on my shoulder and wants to lick my face," said Stuart. "I'll sure miss him if we let him go".

"My favorite is Miss Blueribbon," retorted Pamela. "She's got personality galore."

"Well you can't keep them all," advised Kate.

"You'll keep one and the rest will find new homes," consoled Hayden. "Jenny will have another litter some day".

CHAPTER 4

What's Going On Here?

◇◇◇

Either this box is getting smaller by the day or us are getting bigger. I keep banging up against the sides of the box as Bingo – that's what I call the biggest one of my brothers – dives over two others right into my shoulder. That one knows no boundaries. We need a bigger box!

Mom does cuff him from time to time with that giant paw of hers, smack on his tailbone. He squeals and retreats into a corner where he licks the spot he got slapped. But its only temporary. Now he's back sending another victim head over paws as the rest of us hide behind Mom's large back.

Today a man came and picked us up one at a time, then poking and prodding and flipping us over until I got quite dizzy. No idea what that was all about. He didn't disturb

Mom but each of the rest of us got the same treatment. Must be a ritual of some kind. I even got picked up twice. After that things were pretty quiet in the box until Bingo started running amok again.

It seems the spigot is running dry nowadays. It's hard to get a decent meal from Mom. But we do get a couple of meals a day served in a dish by The lady who cleans up the box and puts new paper down. It's not as good as the stuff that comes out of Mom's spigot but it's more filling. I feel like taking a nap after I wolf down that soft stuff in the dish.

I woke up one day and found it most unusually quiet. I expected Bingo to be challenging one of us to some heavy duty body slams. Looking around there was no sign of Bingo. Gone. I hope he's alright, not hurt in some way. But there's no way to tell. I notice the others in the box are particularly subdued today. Maybe he will come back later.

But that never happened. Actually, a couple of days later another of us went missing. That really scared me. Who would be next? I mean, we really like each other, even Bingo was tolerable some of the time. We loved to play together and being taken away from Mom was scary.

Now two weeks later there are just the three of us. The little skinny one, my sister, the princess and myself. We are allowed out of the box for a few hours in the evening. Mostly we explore looking around at this new landscape of polished and fuzzy floors. I follow my nose, sniffing at anything with a strong aroma. When I find a particularly delectable spot I feel an urge to poop there. That's when I hear a loud shriek and a voice screaming, "Get me the paper towels. He's done it again".

CHAPTER 5

Naming the Dog

"So it's the red puppy, then", mused Stuart.

"That was your decision, Stuart, not mine."

"Well it was him or the princess. She's a lovely bitch and she's going to a lovely family. How could we resist. They fell in love with her and were willing to pay twice what we expected".

Pamela frowned. "Not my choice. She would have been a great show dog."

"We'll never know because they signed a contract that says they can't show her"

"Guess that leaves us with the red dog."

"We can't keep calling him the red dog. We have to give him a name," said Stuart with a grin.

"So let's hear your suggestion".

"Well, I think a dog's name should begin with a B. Like Bowser or Bruno or Bentley."

"How about Barbara or Bella?" chimed Pamela.

"Still harping on letting our little princess go. It's too late Pamela. Think of a B name".

"OK, how about Barley. Like the field across the road".

"That's a ridiculous name."

There was silence for a few moments. Then Pamela jumped up. "I know. Let's call him Barkley."

"That's perfect. But how do you spell that?"

"B A R K L E Y, of course".

"How about B A R K – L E E? Perfect for a dog and so sophisticated."

"Perfect" echoed Pamela.

The next day they started looking for an experienced trainer for Bark-Lee. There were few to choose from in town. Several were already busy or were too expensive for the Campbells. It finally came down to Jim Haskell or Lucretia Borden. But then they learned that Jim had been admitted to the hospital for major surgery and looking forward to a long rehabilitation before resuming his career as a dog trainer.

That left Lucretia, a waspish woman with a short fuse but a reputation as an excellent trainer. Unfortunately her personality had earned her the nickname of The Terrier Terror. She had been around Staffordshire Terriers, otherwise known as Pit Bulls, so long she had begun to resemble the breed.

The Campbells made an appointment for Lucretia to meet their dog. The meeting did not go well.

CHAPTER 6

An Unpleasant Encounter

◇◇◇

This is shocking. Every few days one of us goes missing. A hand reaches into the box and picks another of us – but never me - and that's the last I see of him. Now I'm all alone with Mom. Of course I do get to run around the house and now, occasionally, I'm allowed on the grass in the back yard. I think they prefer that I poop there but I do have an indoor accident from time to time.

I miss my playmates and wonder when it's going to be my turn to be picked up and shipped away. Frankly I'm scared to death. Where will I be taken? Will there be food? Is there going to be somebody to play with? Poor Mom looks sad with nobody to lick or discipline. I think she misses us although we turned out to be quite a handful towards the end.

I'm given toys but I would rather play with someone who likes to roll around the floor and chase me or vise versa. I shouldn't complain. Now I get all the attention.

We had a visitor today, a lady with a face like week old dog food. Her hair was the color of the sky before a storm. Her clothes looked like she got dressed in the basement with the lights off. No, please not this one! I wont go home with her. I'll hide under the sofa. I'll dig a hole in the back yard and crawl inside.

She leaned over the box and scooped me up. Goodbye Mom. I promise to be a good dog. I'll probably never see you again.

Then Lucretia, I heard her called Lucretia, put me down and started to examine me. First she pried open my mouth and with her fingers checked out all my teeth. Then she went to my other end and picked up my tail. How humiliating. I tried to put my tail down to cover my bottom but she rudely lifted it again and ran her hands over my belly ... and more.

Then she took a leash out of her bag and snapped it on my collar. I locked my four paws rigid and refused to move. Lucretia tugged and I skidded forward a few feet. "This one's got a stubborn streak," she said, "but I can handle him". She tugged again. My collar tightened and I felt I would choke. I tried to bark but only a weak little yip escaped through my constricted throat. I was sure Lucretia was intent on torturing me even before taking me to her home.

But then she picked me up and placed me back in the box with Mom. What a relief. That was close. Obviously Lucretia was done with me. Maybe I was not her type or maybe I had shown that she could not mess with me. I feel sorry for the puppy she eventually takes home. For the time being I'm going to curl up next to Mom and take a nap.

CHAPTER 7

The Decision

<><><><><><><><><><><><><><><><><><><><><><><><><><><><><><><>

"So, what do you think, Lucretia?" asked Stuart.

After a long pause Lucretia answered. "Nice looking pup. But he's a stubborn little guy. It's going to take some time and patience to get him to where he will respond properly. And as you know I'm not equipped with either".

"Not very encouraging are you, Lucretia," chimed in Pamela.

"Take it or leave it, " was her terse reply.

"We'll let you know," said Stuart as he escorted Lucretia to the door.

When she was gone the Campbells looked at each other in dismay.

"What a terrible woman," said Pamela.

"But we don't have much choice. Jim's in the hospital and there's nobody else we can hire. If we want to enter Bark-Lee in the Smithtown show we have to start training him now."

"I feel sorry for the dog. He is not going to like Lucretia".

"He looks like a strong puppy. I'm sure he will be alright. And it's only for six months."

Pamela hesitated then nodded her head. "But if I see her abusing our dog, I'll….". Pamela left the rest of the sentence hanging in the air. There was no question about its meaning or her intent.

"I'll call her in the morning. We can set up a schedule. What do you think, three or four times a week?"

Pamela just nodded and went to pick up Bark-Lee. She stroked his soft brown coat, scratched behind his ears and playfully tapped his cold wet nose. In response the puppy licked her fingers. She was sure he would make a fine showdog and win many blue ribbons.

CHAPTER 8

Woe Is Me

◇◇

I looked down at my paws this morning and they are a different color from what I remember. No longer brown I'm beginning to resemble Mom's coat, a sweet caramel hue. I wonder if the others are going through a similar change. Anyway, it suits me fine.

I miss my brothers and sisters. There's nobody to play with. Mom likes to just sit and sleep. Whenever I jump on Mom she just snaps at me and turns her back. Now I'm not so sure she misses all of us. I like to run and jump and chew on whatever anyone has left on the floor. Sometimes it even tastes good like the bone I've been chewing on. It's probably something left over from who knows. I've been chewing on that for a week but it does not seem to be getting any smaller, just softer and more gooy.

My favorite time of the day is when I'm allowed outside. Wow, some incredible smells in the bushes and around the trees. I get the urge to pee whenever I get near that smell. Today I just felt like lifting my rear paw as I got ready to pee. It's so much easier that way.

Every other day Lucretia comes over and I have to go with her for an hour. She's a monster. I can't play or do crazy thing like spinning around chasing my tail when I'm with her. Not even lying around napping. It's go, go, go all the time. I get bathed once a week and then groomed. That is she runs a brush through my hair and then a comb, none too gently. It feels like my hair is being pulled out of my skin and it hurts. She brushes my teeth with some sort of gritty gunk. Once in a while she clips my nails, all twenty of them.

Lucretia takes me for walks through the woods for about an hour. I like that but it's always on a leash. Like I said, I like to run and how far can you run when you are tied to a short tether. Last week I saw my first squirrel. I took off after it but got no more than three feet before my collar tightened and Lucretia pulled me back. Since then I've seen several squirrels and even a rabbit. I don't know what it is but when I see a small furry animal I get this power surge and my paws begin to churn. I don't hate those critters, I just want to chase them. But since they can climb trees or disappear into a hole in the ground I don't expect the chase would last too long. Still, I wonder if maybe I could climb a tree too. Maybe with practice.

I'm beginning to hate Lucretia. The only pleasant part of being around her is when she gives me liver treats. But those pieces are so tiny that it would take a whole bunch to satisfy me. The treats are rewards but I have to work for them, doing what it is she is teaching me to do. I get so excited when I see her reaching into her bag of treats that I jump straight up off the ground. That's when she puts the treats back into the bag until I sit perfectly still.

I would like to train her to stop being such a witch.

CHAPTER 9

The Smithtown Dogshow

Pamela and Stuart drove to Smithtown for the annual dog show. Bark-Lee made the trip in his crate which was firmly tied down on the floor of their van. Lucretia had told them that she would meet them for breakfast at 9. She would be bringing all the paraphernalia that was required to prepare the dog. Since the breed would not be judged until 2 o'clock there was plenty of time for grooming and practice gaiting, showing off how the dog can run.

That also gave the Campbells time to work up a really heavy nervous panic. Lucretia's fees had been substantial. Would it all be worth it? Would Bark-Lee become a star? He certainly looked good. Yesterday he had had his last bath and haircut. Outwardly he looked great. But this was his first show and who can tell what the dog was feeling inside. Seeing all those dogs at the show might spook him with unforeseen consequences.

"So you think he's ready, Lucretia?" asked Stuart.

"Never can tell. He's been a little twitchy the last few days. I can't find anything wrong with him. How is his appetite? You can tell if something is wrong with a dog if he's not eating properly."

"He's eating alright but taking his time. Not gobbling down his food the way he used to," said Pamela.

"He certainly has a mind of his own. Not an easy dog to train, I must say," offered Lucretia with a scowl. " I have two other dogs that I'm handling so if you will excuse me I've got to run."

And she was gone.

Pamela looked tense. "I don't think that was a good match. Bark-Lee always had to be coaxed out of the door when she came over to pick him up."

"Remember, we had no choice," said Stuart. "Let's go check out the competition."

So off they went to look over the terriers who were being pampered to photo perfection. Most of the dogs seemed to be energized, while exhausted trainers and breeders tried to keep them under control while blow drying their hair into a wheat colored fluff.

That competition is going to be tough to beat, thought

Pamela. The couple wandered back to the café where they drank more coffee which did nothing to calm their nerves.

It was almost two o'clock when the Campbells sat down at ringside to watch their beloved Bark-Lee face his first judge, a middle aged matron with two chins, bird's nest hair and close set eyes. But they had a friendly twinkle in them as she greeted the handlers and their dogs, nine of them, and directed them to line up facing her. Bark-Lee was the next to last dog in line.

The judge examined each dog carefully. Then watched as they walked in a circle around the ring. Now it was Bark-Lee's turn. The judge felt the dog's back, shoulders and head. She was about to open his mouth to check his teeth when Lucretia said. "This is his first show. He's a little skittish. Do you mind if I hold his mouth open while you look."

"No. Go ahead. That's OK with me," the judge responded.

Lucretia reached to part the dog's lips. What happened next shocked everyone. The judge let out a hair raising scream, snatched her hand away from Bark-Lee's head and reached for the towel draped over a ringside chair. Blood dripped from her wounded hand and soaked the towel. Lucretia stood stunned having never witnessed anything like this in ten years of handling dogs.

The Campbells ran into the ring. Pamela picked Bark-Lee up, tried to calm him down. The dog was trembling, with fright or fury she could not tell.

"He bit me," yelled the judge, a fact that was obvious to all. "Get him out of here".

The Campbells needed no urging. They ran back to their van, placed Bark-Lee in his crate and drove away exceeding the speed limit all the way home.

CHAPTER 10

The Bite

◇◇◇

I'm in my crate in the van and I'm thinking, this is unusual. The bath yesterday. I wasn't due for my next one for another week. I keep track of these things seeing as how that's not exactly my favorite thing. And we leave the house at the crack of dawn. Something weird is going down. Maybe they are taking me to the vet. I hate those shots he gives me.

Besides the pain in my gums is not getting any better. I was chewing on that table leg when I felt this sharp pain in my mouth. Must have been a splinter I picked up. Better stick to rawhide and bones from now on. Table legs don't agree with me and I get shouted at when they catch me chomping on them.

We're pulling up to some kind of large shed. I don't

like the looks of this place. Maybe they decided they don't want me any more and are taking me to a dog market to sell me. That's probably the reason I got that bath yesterday. And that's why there are all those dogs in crates out there. Woe is me!

Oh, there's Lucretia so maybe I'm wrong. Maybe this is a big dog party where we get treats for good behavior. Lucretia looks her usual sourpuss self. Nothing new here. I'm used to all that grooming, shpritzing, combing, blow drying and smoothing. Now she's getting the toothbrush out. Watch out Lucretia for that splinter.

Ow, that hurt. You do that one more time I'll give you pain you wont forget, my fair lady. How much longer am I going to have to put up with this? Fine, I'm ready. Let the party begin.

So now they have us lined up. All those dogs look just like me. I wonder if any of my brothers and sisters are here. I wouldn't recognize them and they wouldn't recognize me. But I would love to have a play date with any one of them.

The one in front of me smells of rotting leaves. Delicious. Maybe I can get closer to her bottom and get a good, hearty sniff. Darn it Lucretia. Stop pulling on the leash. I'm choking to death. Then I notice that the one behind me is giving my bottom a lot of attention.

We keep moving forward. Maybe when I get to the head of the line there will be treats. I'm there now but no treats yet. Instead a rather large lady is feeling me all over.

Stop that! It tickles. Now Lucretia is opening my mouth…. Stop that, Lucretia. …I warned you….You asked for it….

Why is the chubby lady screaming? Doggone it I bit her instead of Lucretia. I'm so sorry, I'm so sorry, I'm so sorry. I'm shaking all over. And here comes Pamela and Stuart and they are picking me up. Please take me to my crate. This is so terrible. I'm so sorry.

CHAPTER 11

A Second Chance?

◇◇

Pamela and Stuart sat in silence. Neither one wanted to discuss the incident at the dog show. Bark-Lee was curled up in his crate. He seemed just as shaken as his owners. Finally Stuart broke the silence.

"I have never seen a dog attack a judge like that. Maybe we should just sell him as a pet because I doubt he will ever appear in a show ring again."

"First I want to know what caused him to react like that," said Pamela. "Then we can decide what to do."

"I doubt that would make any difference but go ahead take him to the vet tomorrow."

The vet found the problem but it was too late. A week

later the Campbells received a letter from the American Kennel Club. Pamela brought it in from the mailbox but refused to open it. She gave it to Stuart. He read it to her.

"Dear Mr. and Mrs. Campbell, The AKC has been informed that your dog, namely Bark-Lee is guilty of attacking a judge which caused her pain and suffering and a trip to the local hospital emergency room. Due to this unfortunate incident at the Smithtown dog show your dog Bark-Lee is banned from further competition in the show ring. This prohibition extends to all dog shows throughout the United States. We are sorry to have to take this action but we must protect our judges."

Pamela was devastated. She had placed so much hope in Bark-Lee. He was such a sweet dog, so friendly, so happy. Of course she suspected what had caused him to bare his teeth but that was not going to make any difference now.

Stuart sighed. "You know that Bark-Lee is the best looking dog we ever had," he said.

"That's true", answered Pamela, "but so what?"

"So, how about we appeal the decision. Tell them what the vet told us, about the splinter in his gum."

"It wont make any difference. They'll never believe us," snapped Pamela.

"They don't have to believe us. I have it in writing from the vet. Look Pamela, there's no harm in trying".

So the Campbells filed an appeal and surprisingly they

received a letter asking them to appear before the Appeals Committee to state their case.

Three weeks later Pamela and Stuart drove to Smithtown to present reasons why Bark-Lee should be reinstated and allowed to appear in future dog shows. The Appeals Committee chairman, Mr. Clark, looked over the documents they had presented, coughed several times, then put the papers aside.

"Dr. Hayworth, your veterinarian, states that he removed a large splinter from your dog's lower gum. Apparently this caused him some discomfort. And as a result he bit the judge who was examining him.'

"That's right", said Stuart. "We also believe that he had no intention of biting the judge. You see it was his handler, Lucretia Borden, who was prying his mouth open at the time. Over the course of the last few months Lucretia has been rather strict with the dog and we got the impression that Bark-Lee did not take kindly to her harsh discipline".

"My committee is aware of Ms. Borden's methods. Some complaints have been filed but she has done nothing illegal or unethical. Still I can understand that your dog might have mistakenly bit the judge."

A ray of hope lit the room. Maybe, maybe, Mr. Clark would be sympathetic to their appeal.

"Still," went on Clark, "you should have been aware of

the dog's predicament. And most assuredly Ms. Borden. Before you take a dog into the show ring he must be examined thoroughly for any medical problem."

Just as suddenly that ray dimmed and disappeared.

Clark fell silent. He was obviously considering their case before making a final decision. He looked up and announced.

"This is a promising dog, so the judge tells me. It was his first show and there is a plausible reason why he acted the way he did. I do not want to ruin a young dog's career. I will approve the appeal and reinstate your dog. Of course if this happens again Bark-Lee will never see a show ring again."

The Campbells rose, shook Mr. Clark's hand vigorously and thanked him. Then they ran out of his office and raced home.

Pamela and Stuart were giddy with excitement. Although they had hoped for a favorable verdict they had little confidence that it would happen. They had not thought very far ahead. What would be their next step? Who would they engage to train and handle Bark-Lee?

"Naturally we can't use Lucretia again," mused Stuart. "And I don't think we can afford another trainer now."

Pamela was silent. She knew the family finances were not in good shape. It was doubtful that anyone would take on Bark-Lee on their budget and his record of assaulting a judge.

Suddenly she exclaimed, "I know. Why don't I train him?"

"You can't be serious Pam."

"I am very serious. I have always wanted to train dogs. And this is my chance. I've read lots of books on dog training. My friend Tammy will help me. She's retired but she was once a handler at the Westminster Dog Show in New York. You know, the biggest dog show in the country. I'm sure I can do it."

"No question Bark-Lee loves you and will do anything you ask. But it's a big commitment of your time."

After some further discussion Stuart reluctantly went along with Pamela's enthusiastic decision to become Bark-Lee's trainer and dog handler.

CHAPTER 12
Hard Work

I came home and spent the next three days curled up next to Mom until Stuart took me to the vet to check me out. I'm glad he did because my gum was hurting me badly. The vet removed the splinter from my mouth. What a relief. Now I can eat properly and you know how important dog chow is to a puppy.

But there was still that awful scream from that woman with the double chin. I'm sorry. I meant to snap at Lucretia because she was hurting me. In any case Lucretia was always harsh. I don't think she likes dogs at all.

But suddenly Pamela is spending a lot more time with me. Like Lucretia she is teaching me but much more gently.

She also talks sweetly to me and I give her licks to tell her how much I love her.

We go for long walks in the woods. Lots of squirrels for me to chase. Sorry, I haven't caught one yet. I'm sure I will one of these days.

There seems to be some sort of exercise I'm supposed to learn, like standing on a mat, absolutely still. When I do that I get a treat. Pamela insists that my paws be straight, exactly the same distance apart every time. When I am on the leash I am to trot along at the same speed as Pamela. When I am picked up I get a little dizzy, but regardless I must never snap at anyone for any reason.

Pamela is very generous with treats. Liver bits. Delicious. It really gets my attention but often she just waves those tidbits in front of my face without letting me eat. That's cruel. Lunging for the treats is not allowed. I'm supposed to wait until she pops it into my mouth.

And the baths. Not once a month like before, but every week. And then brush, brush, brush until my hair sparkles, my beard flows and my paws have a butternut sheen.

So I'm wondering what this is all about. I thought that the double chinned lady was giving a party for us dogs or at least a swell play date. Now I think that is probably not the case. Today Pamela put a picture of a dog who looks just like me in front of my crate. He is standing with the lady with the double chin with a large silver cup and a blue ribbon. What does that mean? Certainly not a party. There's only one dog.

I'm thinking that maybe this is a game with one winner. Could that be me? Is that why all my brothers and sisters were sent to new homes and I was the only one who stayed with Mom and Pamela and Stuart? And then I bit the double chinned lady who was going to give me a blue ribbon and a shiny cup to eat out of. I am going to have to do a lot better next time. Next time is coming soon I think. Time to look and act my best so I can make Pamela proud of me.

CHAPTER 13

A Second Try at Stardom

"One more week, Pamela, and it's show time". Stuart was brimming with enthusiasm and confidence.

"Thank goodness," replied Pamela, "I couldn't keep this up much longer. The dog is exhausting me".

"But it's done you some good too. I bet you lost at least 20 lbs. in the last six months."

"I'm going to have to buy a new outfit for the show next week. My closet is full of clothes that just hang on me."

"Get yourself something bright and glitzy. The judges will like that."

"I'm sure they would. But it's Bark-Lee I want them to watch."

Stuart thought for a moment. "Do you think he is ready?

"Yes. He seems to have found his rhythm lately. Ever since I put that photo of the winner of last year's show in front of his crate. He keeps looking at it as if he understands. Maybe it inspires him because he is as ready as I had hoped for."

Then she added, "Those three mile hikes through the woods, those obedience exercises, that new diet we put him on. I would say he's ready."

"You've done a great job, Pamela," said Stuart admiringly.

She was tired but happy. "You know Lucretia will be there. She has a new dog, a female, name of Guinivere of Camelot. People call her Ginny. Ginny won two Best in Shows last year and five Best in Breeds. Tough competition for Bark-Lee."

Just then Bark-Lee walked in from the kitchen. Stuart looked at him with a big grin on his face. "Are you ready for Showtime?" Bark-Lee wagged his tail as if he understood the question.

"Ready for his run, more likely," said Pamela as she hoisted herself off the couch and reached for the dog's leash.

Stuart wheeled the small trolley from the parking lot into the arena. The passenger in the crate on top of the trolley was the dog the Campbells had pinned their hopes on. Bark-Lee looked as splendid as they had ever seen him. His lavish caramel colored coat shone, every hair in place.

No need to have him walk through the wet, leaf strewn parking lot and then have to comb out his paws again.

Other owners, breeders, handlers were crowding into the space set aside for prepping their dogs. Dogs of more than a hundred breeds. Some Pamela and Stuart had never heard of. The place was a bedlam of nervous people and barking canines. In the middle of the arena were four fenced in rings where dogs of various breeds were competing for prizes before the judges. The Campbells found a spot to park their crate. They opened its gate and out stepped Bark-Lee, a truly princely looking dog.

Pamela went to work, brushing out any matts that had developed during the car ride from their home. She sprayed some water over his paws and combed them out. Then straightened his beard. Finally she smoothed out his tail with a damp cloth. In response he wagged it enthusiastically. He was ready!

At exactly noon Pamela strode into ring #4. She wore a midnight blue, ankle length dress, to set off the dog's sunny caramel colored hair. On her right sleeve she wore the armband she had been given on registration. Number 17; it had always been her lucky number. Maybe, just maybe, this would be her and Bark-Lee's lucky day.

Pamela joined a line of twelve dogs, all terriers . She looked up to see Lucretia holding Ginny on a short leash just in front of her.

CHAPTER 14

Showtime!

<><><><><><><><><><><><><><><><><><><><><><><><><><><><><><>

It's like last year except bigger. All kinds. Big and shaggy, tiny and smooth. And everything in between. I'm going to have to try my best to win that bowl and that ribbon. I just hope that double chinned lady doesn't show up. Would she recognize me and toss me out. I'll let Pamela worry about that.

I know, I know, I have to be on my best behavior. But with all these dogs to play with it's hard to stand still and get brushed for the twentieth time today. At least I look like a dog. Some of them have the weirdest shape, like they collided with a lawnmower.

It's all so overwhelming. I wish we could get this over

with and go home. Who needs a silver bowl. Mine is just as good. Food tastes the same.

Pamela is picking me off the table and putting me on the floor. This is it. I'm ready …. I think. We are heading for a ring along with several more familiar looking dogs. They could easily be my brothers and sisters. As we enter the ring I get a wiff of the most heavenly aroma. It's coming from that dog in front of me. It's a girl dog and she is the most beautiful thing I have ever seen.

I'm going to wag my tail to attract her attention. Pamela, please stop holding my tail. I'm trying to get her to turn around. She must be someone special because when she entered the ring there was loud clapping and yelling. Nobody clapped when I walked in except Stuart and a couple of Pamela's friends.

Pamela is speaking softly in my ear. She is trying to calm me down. But that aroma from the girl dog is driving me crazy. She never turns around, but her handler does. Oh my goodness, it's Lucretia. What to do.

The person in charge is a short, gray haired man who walks down the line touching each of us but very gently. I like him immediately. More important, does he like me? Now his hands are all over me. Please don't do that sir. It tickles. If I was not a dog I would be giggling.

Now Pamela has me on a very short leash and is taking me for a short walk around the ring. The short man must like what he saw because he asked Pamela to step on the side. I see Lucretia's dog has been selected too along with two others. The man keeps walking between us, tickling me again, smoothing out 'she-who-I-have-fallen-in-love-with'. Every time he goes to her the people around the ring clap and cheer loudly. When he walks back to me hardly anyone reacts. I'm getting upset here. Pamela is breathing hard. Even Lucretia is getting nervous.

Finally the short man walks over to the long table in the ring to write something down. He picks up a ribbon, points to Pamela and says "First", then at Lucretia's dog and says "Second". Pamela picks me up and squeezes me so tight I think I'm going to burst. I give a sharp bark which convinces Pamela to put me down. She lets go of my leash and in the next second I'm muzzle to muzzle with my new love.

Here come the photographers. They take a few pictures of the two of us but Pamela drags me away to pose with my silver bowl and blue ribbon. Of course Pamela invites Stuart to come into the ring and the three of us smile for the photographers. Not sure anyone can see me smiling, but I really am.

CHAPTER 15

The Perfect Match

◇◇

Pamela could not understand why the judge seemed unable to make up his mind. He bent down to examine Ginny, then walked over to Bark-Lee to feel his thighs. Then retreated back to Ginny. It was intolerable to be kept in suspense like this. I'll be happy with second place, she thought, just get this over with. Finally the judge walked over to the table, picked up a blue ribbon and pointed at her. She thought she would faint. Then Lucretia came over and extended her hand.

"Congratulations Pamela. I always knew that pup of yours had it in him to win. He just needed a little more discipline. Let's talk later." And she was gone.

They met again in the parking lot.

"I noticed that Bark-Lee showed a lot of interest in Ginny. She is coming into season in a couple of weeks. Her owner does not plan on showing her again and so if you, and Bark-Lee agree we could make a match between the two dogs," suggested Lucretia.

"That's a fine proposition, don't you think Pamela," said Stuart.

"Yes", answered Pamela. "With two such beautiful dogs, can you imagine the puppies they would have."

EPILOGUE
Six Months Later

Bark-Lee and Ginny produced their first litter of nine puppies – five girls and four boys. Three of that litter would win blue ribbons and one would be the Best in Show at a major dog show on the West Coast. A year and a half later they became parents again. This time it was seven puppies – two girls and five boys. Within two years one of those puppies was invited to the Westminster Dog Show, the biggest and most famous in the United States.

Ginny and Bark-Lee saw each other in the park frequently. They may have discussed what they thought about Lucretia or talked about puppy problems. We will never know.

ACKNOWLEDGMENT:
THE PUBLICATION OF THIS BOOK OWES
SIGNIFICANT ASSISTANCE FROM MY FRIEND
OF 30 YEARS, NICK GREGORIC.